The Burning Cone

GEORGE MACBETH

The Burning Cone

MACMILLAN

Published by
MACMILLAN AND CO LTD
Little Essex Street London WC2
and also at Bombay Calcutta and Madras
Macmillan South Africa (Publishers) Pty Ltd
Johannesburg
The Macmillan Company of Australia Pty Ltd Melbourne
The Macmillan Company of Canada Ltd Toronto

PRINTED IN GREAT BRITAIN BY
THE BOWERING PRESS PLYMOUTH

ACKNOWLEDGEMENTS

Some of these poems have appeared in the following magazines: *Ambit, Outposts, The Poetry Review, The Southern Review (U.S.A.).* One of them, 'A Death', was a Sceptre Press pamphlet. To the editors of these magazines, and to the publishers of Sceptre Press books, my acknowledgements are due.

CONTENTS

I	A Light in Winter	3
II	A Death	21
	To a Slow Drum	23
	The Snow Leopard	28
III	In the Dark	33
	On the Thunersee	38
IV	To Autumn	47
	To a Nightingale	50
	On Melancholy	55
	To a Grecian Urn	58
V	A Christmas Ring	65
	Notes	73

the burning cone,
      wherein all enter,
to die, or be reborn

I

A LIGHT IN WINTER

I

She sat, legs gripping, eyes
Upturning, in the front row.
As he spoke,
Reeling through Vitruvius, she was vague
And nagging in his back mind.
Then she asked
Something, out-urging slurred words.
Sharp
In their intending, he took in high boots,
Voice, twisted fingers.
As he answered, she
Hooked like an anchor, dragging at his groin
And brain.
It ended, and the audience clashed
Towards winter traffic.
As they broke the street,
Rain-lashed, with black cars shining, she
Hunched in her cords, mauve, belted.
Her wet hair
Framed the bark eyes, distended, shawled
In the mist of drug-light.
As wrecked wood, she dredged
Through tangling weeds, dense people.
He caught up,
Switched to her step, spoke to her sidelong face
Against the crowd.
Impulsive, as she watched him, he
Took her arm, urged her through a glass door, leaned
With her at a bar.
Used to nothing, she
Tested his knuckles, gripped at them, drank gin
Through smoke and darkness, dodging questions.
In

The taxi later, tongued in leather, lipped
As they rounded Hyde Park Corner, her
High legs eased, fingers opened.
                              As they rode
Against each other's bodies, briefly, he
Sensed her powered absence.
                              When she slouched out, near
Where she was living, with her number in
His calf-skin book, he waved, once.
                              She strudged in,
Clenched in her coat, stiff, man-like.
                              When he wrote
Arranging meetings, she was ill
And couldn't see him.
                              When she wrote back, he
Watched the blue, sick strokes wrangle on the page,
Sexed, wild.
                              As the need to see her fixed him tighter, he
Forgot his wife, job, only saw hard lust
Forged in a pouch for spending.
                              As he sketched
Through polished silence, or ate breakfast, poised
In jangling talk, he trembled.
                              In his bed,
Beside the jewel of his calm, his wife,
He felt an absorbed wilting.
                              So she came,
Flown from her darkness to his light.

II

                              At the place
Agreed, and in the time, oblivious to
His laid work, he sat waiting.
                              In his mind
The tower he was building dwindled.
                              When she knocked,
Clutching a doll, in dark shades, barefoot, he
Shocked his firm nerves to ready taking.

4

                              By
The steel green cases, chilled, in half-dimmed space,
They kissed, holding.
                    In soft abandon, wrapped
Over a tautness of luxurious doubt,
Her mind enriched him.
                         So they came, hands held,
To a glowing room.
                    Men bowing, instruments
Of a bored thunder, lightened.
                         By the sheets
Of traced façades, pinned elevations, tricks
And fancies of irrelevant ornament, some
Shimmered in glass, charmed, winsome.
                                   Their
Willowy consorts, offered mistresses,
Pawed, shouldered, flouncing.
                         He
Faced them, detached, observed her.
                              When she stood,
Silent, in others talking, her feet splayed,
Strange, goose-like.
                    In their eating, tumbling prawns
With a barbed fork, hot feeling found
Its symptoms.
                    They came out soon, cooled, and walked
To where she lived, hired attic.
                              In bare lust
His teeth rattled, as a skull's.
                              Her shift slid up
And over null bones, shielded.
                              Muscular
And flexing, on that sewn quilt, she
Opened her purse of illness.
                         As bent legs
Vaulted, spare arches into darkness, she
Enfranchised him in all she felt.
                         So soothed
Into her world of subtle blurring, he

                                             5

Straddled, half-dreaming.
                         Where her curved ways led
Him on, he walked in vigilant watching, ranged
Over her hills, through forests, by a stream
To the high castle.
                         In those crumbled foreign walls,
Echoing with bats and strange horns, he
Reached the jarl's table.
                         There he sat and ate,
Lifting the encrusted cup.
                         And in his dream,
Swirled in an aura of sweet scents, he dived
Into a dream of dreams.
                         Lazily, whales
And sharks moved, reeling through green weeds,
Falling and killing.
                         When he woke, or lost both, they
Gasped in a sweat of cold, wind hissing in
Through an open window.
                         It was all
It never was.

III

                         Low strangeness hung
Over his thoughts for long days.
                         She
Was in him, of him.
                         Under her thick spell
The arts of Christmas withered.
                         Her gloss card
With a black smile, some negro, and her news
Of quarrels, mess, bored ailments, filled
His days with clear light.
                         In exchange, his grooved
Whirling disc drove her furies back.
                         For hours
One night, that organ music ripped slick wings
To shreds.

6

                    She moved in coolness to a cave
Where someone waited.
                         Slow and cold,
Again those wings flicked.
                              He was too far in
His own concerns to care, though.
                                   What she had
Was all the need of months for fullness, life
In the same room, a man's laugh.
                                  He could help
Only a little, less than he knew.
                              So she
Planned a disaster, helpless.
                              In the quick
Under the covers, even as they humped
Like spoons, in close liaison, it all soured
To a head.
                    One night she never came
At the known time.
                         Then later, they
Rang in the gross night.
                              She was back
With slit wrists in a locked room.

IV

                              As he read
The brutal card that told him, bolted in
A men's-room cubicle, crude scalding drops
Melted the burned ink.
                         In his eyes
Her passion misted, emptied.
                              In dour grief
He folded what she sent, signed flowing letters, then
Graved them in memory, flushed them.
                                   As he sat
Again beside that high glass, turning lead
In his poised fingers, he could see her arms,
Gashed, scarred.

7

In the watched room,
She crouched against the wall.
On a mattress, rigid
In locked fear, she spent hours.
The words rose back
Out of the blue square, swollen, blurred,
Thrashing his calm.
Day after day
Caged in that lift, as in his own taut mind,
He rose up, tried to see her.
She was tired
And seeing no-one.
In four weeks she wrote once
In sprawled mauve, Japanese felt-pen.
Illegible signs,
Frail, spidery.
He read them, wrote back, hauled
Into a pitiable chaos of longing.
Gorged
On dreams of flesh and spending, he
Showed his remoteness.
In drab hints
Noted, and swallowed, his wife grasped, and hoped,
Still, it was office trouble.
On the screen
Others played out their drama.
Here it swayed
As a slow weight.
In thin poise, to and fro,
Their union clicked and held,
Saturate with the oils of mercy.
If
Her mind risked thinking he was faithless, she
Jibbed at the huge truth.
Soon
Their bodies would resume.
And so the year
Edged to the raw Spring.

V

There, one iron day
She came out.
In the woods and galleries
He watched her grow back.
With her blooded arms
Under his own, he reached for softer passion, touched
Her delicate centre.
Where before, their minds
Fused in a drenched rush, now
They scorched in milder fire.
At Putney once
They strolled in prickling sunlight, spitting pips
Of grapes in the river.
Tanned by inward light,
Her pitted face, pinched by the winter heat,
Faltered in smiling, as they paused.
By an oak,
Racked into hollow fretwork, she stretched up
And kissed his neck.
He touched her razored arms,
Grown to the tree's heart.
So their pact was sealed
In hungry April.
How the sadder change occurred,
And moved the cured lust from the tender love
Into excess of dullth, he never knew,
Or faced.
For her perhaps the nub
Of change was in the stars, or in her blood,
Still blending, as do oils.
However it
Happened, it did so.
As the year burned, all
Settled, as on an isled sea.
Stretching to
Some edge of merging, their horizon calm
Of easy loving fooled both.

9

If she fretted, he
Bathed in a sweet lagoon of touching, gulfed
In swathing lust.
She grew remote, unpurged,
Ill at ease.
Each night, when he rose, dressed
And left her in the low hours, edged with fear,
She felt resentment.
That first need
For someone sane receded.
In her healed
Half-grown new mind, a drive came for a friend
Less normal, wilder.
What she needed now
Was someone like herself.
Some final test
Of mended fibre.
So the other, when he came
In burned late August, was
Inevitable, a laboratory.

VI

They had both
Gone to a stadium.
In her sheen of PVC
And plastic visor, she was modern, hip
And cured.
As an attractive decoy, she
Lolled with her legs up.
Hinting boredom, by
Her shaken hair, she caught eyes.
Under the dome
In hectic arc-light, they engaged.
White cars
Raced in the stench of violent action, wrenched
Round and round a firm track.
He sat
Locking cold numbers on a board.

10

As each
Ripped and performed, he clocked them.
A man leaned
In easy leather, awkward, shy,
Offering her a cigarette.
In the glare
Of all those egos, flowered silk and sound,
He was relaxed.
She talked
Into his ear, laughed, strained with words
On the board.
For Christ's sake take me home
And screw me, man.
He stayed with numbers, times,
Not caring.
So the paired scales hitched and slid,
Upsetting them.
As iron, she withdrew,
Freed from the lodestone.
As he went to wash,
Leaving his metal case with her, she clutched
His arm, pleaded, said not now.
So he went
And came back with her gone.
So many times
In later weeks he was to feel the same,
This jealous bile, frustrated anger, hate
For a man's hair.
That first night, shivering,
He drove home.
In the bedroom, in the dark,
Undressing softly, he heard his wife breathe
In uneasy sleep.
Not noticing, deaf
In his pain, he crept in, tried to join her.
Crushed
In still hate, he sank under.
Turning, he splayed flat
On his belly, slewing rucked sheets.

11

B

                              In the heat,
Squalid with rumpled, anxious dreams, he heard
Rain, ramming the roof.
                         Outside, thin birds
With breaking feathers, lifted, hurled
Oceans of muscle into bald air.
                              As it burst
Through violence of pent wind, each was culled
Into a winnowing of silence.
                         Furrowed earth
Eased with its worms.
                         Black slugs lurched under leaves
Rustling huge drops off.
                         As he lay, he felt
Raw tension settle into troubled shaking, pin
Stiff nerve-ends.
                         Quivering, stilled,
He urged hot lips against the head-board.
                                   His wife turned
Out of some dream, half-crying, rising, lapsed
Once again, as a fish would, swept
In the down-draught, to the bottom.
                              Then he slept,
Not meaning to, but tired.
                         And the storm rolled
All night.

VII

          In the morning, he rose, drove
To the tower site, over wet roads.
                         When he rang,
She sounded strange, numb.
                         In the glass box
Over his papers, he was trembling, taut
As he fixed a meeting.
                         Under the crane,
Watching the rubble swung, he saw her face
Teeming with dark fish, all day.

12

Tense, at eight,
He collected her, raced through the savage park
To a lonely place.
　　　　　　Against the wheel,
Pressing his head, he rested.
　　　　　　　　With her knees
Locked back, hair swung off, hands clawed, she
Groped in her pain to help him.
　　　　　　　　　As the cars
Rocked past in flooding summer, singed with
　　leaves
Out of the failing light, he saw the hands
Grip in the clock, stir, threaten.
　　　　　　　　　As the sour
Injustice hit him, he heaved up, surged, struck
Her bare face, forced his whickering hand
Against her clasped legs.
　　　　　　　In the untidy riot of clutched
Struggle in awkward space, clenched, hurt
And screaming, they scracked over chromium, glass,
Wood, stewed
In a hash of envious violence.
　　　　　　　　Then half-spilled
Through stupid angles, postures of abused
Self-hatred, they felt sex lift, steal
Into the crannies of cramped anger.
　　　　　　　　Leaning, strained
Over the leatherette arm-rest, they bunched up
In one seat, forged a broached umbrella, crammed
Each other.
　　　　　　When the tumbled rush had passed
In white flights to the far horizon, they
Broke into two, lay over.
　　　　　　　All
Mended for moments, it was closeness in
Their globe.
　　　　　　His pride secured, he rode
Into the pleasure of remembered hope,
Forgave, and laughed.

13

She kissed him, and the stars
Crept into fresh positions, crouched for war
And evacuation.
They drove back
In each other's arms, knowing the falls was near
And would overwhelm them.
That was the last night
They even touched.

VIII

Far away, calm at home
In a mews yard in Hampstead, hard
In grease-pocked overalls, the blond boy worked
Racing in neutral.
Beside his door, high gloss
Shone on a bared, smear engine, moving parts
With inexorable power.
His oil-stained hands,
Uneven ways, washed straw hair, drew
Her into promises, cracked vows.
As he
Sketched late, at the point block, waiting, she
Never arrived, though swearing to.
One time
He took it, smiled.
The next, he felt hate stir
And thin despair flick.
So the autumn drained
Into a vacuum of envy, knowing love
Grate in its last few grains.
One evening, working late
Under the painful strip-lights, he
Dreamed in a waking terror.
He had gone
To see her, found them both there.
They were lax
After love-making.

14

When he came in, they
Woke, and then giggled, flaunting their bare skin,
Erect and goose-fleshed in his hampered face,
Famished with jealousy.
                              So he would seize
And work with scissors, hacking at their forks
With accurate hands.
                              Watch blood spurt, laughter split
Into a tattered agony of pleading.
                                                    Stop,
For God's sake, stop.
                              Then he found his calipers
Driven by white knuckles deep into the board,
And his arm shaking.
                              He unclenched his fist,
Striving to soothe himself.

IX

                              And then,
With no perceptible crisis, while
The chestnut walls burst open, and green mines
Exploded mahogany on gravel, he
Felt a control come.
                              Gradually at first,
Then tauter, with a sense of joy in things,
Love swivelled.
                              In his panelled house,
Dulled with the sound of ghostly breathing, all
The brooches pricked and held still.
                                                    He was lulled
Through grown content, rich pleasures.
                                                    As enwombed,
He lolled in safety, fed and sure.
                                                    His wife,
Salt in a hunger of envenoming tears,
Gathered, using her precious gains.
                                                    As she served
Him toast in a silver dish, hot soup, and kidneys, he

Grew to the will to love her.
                              Once again,
He saw the clean grace in her nose-line, sweep
Of corn-grey hair, and clean clothes.
                                    As she bent
To lift a fallen paper, pain
At so much deceit of such a sure friend sucked
Hot sobs in his throat.
                          He remembered how,
Years back, another veering ended.
                                      In
The flare of trombones it began, with fears
Of marriage breaking, then
A drying started.
                      How, he never knew,
Or couldn't think now, only that it did,
And spread until they parted.
                                  After weeks,
They nudged once, in a fruit-shop.
                                      Meeting her
Over those balls, Corbusier ovals, shapes
And odours of ground, sumptuous plenty, he
Dried like a thrown pip.
                            If love winced in then,
It could now.
                  And this woman, with
The dove's hair, bird of passage, tamed and swollen,
    could
Be where it aimed.
                      As he watched her body sway
In sinuous elegance, a buried lust
Shivered, he touched her.
                              Tangled in their bed,
Under the skeins of tension, wet and sleek
In oils of passion, they could swim,
Each thought, in brine of pity.
                                    So,
As always, in the need to last, alive
In friendship, each accepted what there was,

16

And used it honestly.
                        He turned, and waved
In his mind, to the past.
                        In the office, when,
Days later, truth rang, he was filing.
                                        As
He set the bakelite back in
Its holder, he reflected how it seemed
So small, all bad news.
                        They
Had flown to France.
                        And so it ended, in
One sentence.
                Why it had to, and why then,
He never knew, though knowing.

X

                        Looking out, through
That high glass, lashed with chill sleet, he
Slipped into winter, losing her.
                                Now she
Was all one with the shed seeds, fallen in
Some drift of snow.
                        Drumming the black shell
In its cradle, he began to sketch, eyes blind
With final hail, against the pain-storm.
                                        Fined
Into a second of thin terror, he
Severed it all in flared lines, flowing shapes,
Showing her, what she was.
                                Was there so much
He never knew, in madness?
                                Now,
Under the axe, it seemed so.
                                As he sketched
Blindly, the tower of a stone church, high
On a precipice, overlooking a long drop,
He saw her coming.

                                        17

                              As a black, slight figure, dots
Only, in one far corner, she
Mounted a path towards the light.
                                          A cross
Blazed, with a slung fish on the steeple, Christ
In seaward glory.
                              To that reach of salt and calm,
Lifting a black weight out of nowhere, she
Drove like a lost ship.
                                    Fighting, dying now,
Into a fluxion of tense water, calmed
And still, Narcissus, she was gone.
                                          Then the door
Opened, and his wife entered.
                                          He tore off
The whole sheet, ripped it hard across,
Crunched it in the waste-bin.
                                          He was back
In the plain present.
                              Once again
The ram broke, and across the window sleet
Swept as before, draining the light.
                                    He rose
And took his brief-case, and went home with her,
In a dream of children, running to kiss his hands.

A DEATH

I

His fur
was wet, he must have been out
and sleeping in the rain.
The wet
made little thorn-shapes
on his back, and there were shreds
of pine-twigs in his tail.
I carried him
carefully, away from my body,
so as not to shake him.
The vet
cut a few tufts of hair
from his right shin
with a pair of scissors.
He
asked me to put my thumb
in the joint of his knee
to hold him still.
Then he
injected the green liquid
into his leg, and it
turned red, as
a little blood
was drawn in.
We left him
to be burned.

II

Later,
as we walked across Richmond Green,
the whole sky
glowed flame-red.

                        A jet went over
with a cracked roar.
                        In the noise
and the fire, it was easy
to feel a huge wind
out of his body
                        seared into the air,
and draining away.

Goodbye, Peter.

TO A SLOW DRUM

a stately music

I

Solitary thoughts,
and burial mounds,
begin this dirge,
and mournful sounds.

II

Now to the dead march
troop in twos,
the granite owls
with their *Who Was Who's*,
the bat, and the grave, yew
bear on his wheels,
Tuborg the pig
with his hard wood heels.

III

Gemmed with a dew
of morning tears,
the weeping armadillo
has brought his shears :
the droop-ear dog
and the lion come,
dipping their long waists
to meet the drum.

IV

On the bare chafing-dish
as each one hears,
the grey lead pigs
reverse their spears :

grooved in line,
they show no grief,
grouped above a sere
and yellow leaf,
a tree's life blown
through a crack in the door.

V

Over the red-black
kitchen floor,
Jeremy the spider
stalks to his place,
all eight legs
wet from the waste :
he climbed up the drain
to be here on time.

VI

Now, to the slow
egg-timer's chime,
shiny in state
come things from the grime :
tiny slaters
with wings and hoods,
beetles from the closet
under the stairs :
gashed with sorrow
each fixed eye stares.

VII

Fairbanks crawls
from his winter leaves :
he rubs his eyes
on his prickling sleeves :
rattling his plate
for a sad sound,

his black legs cover
the chill ground
at a fair speed :
he creeps to our need.

VIII

Now the hall resounds
to the tread of toes
as each one gathers,
and the crowd grows :
broken-spirited,
the bears upstairs
troop to the banisters
and droop their ears :
the brown one squats,
glum cheeks in his paws,
the blue one strums
a melancholy string.

IX

From all feasts of fish
he wove good fur:
alas, no fish
stale death can deter.

X

As the drum beats,
the long cortège
winds to the attic
as towards the stage :
some hop and skip,
some crawl or run,
the sad music
holds every one :

crouched by the window
all weep to view
Peter, poor Peter,
drift up the flue.

XI

Now, all together
they chant his dirge,
grouped by the ledge
where the chimneys merge.

XII

Peter, salt Peter,
fish-eating cat,
feared by the blackbird,
stung by the gnat,
wooden-spider collector,
lean as a rat,
soon you shall fall
to a fine grey fat.

XIII

Peter, salt Peter,
drift into the wind,
enter the water
where all have sinned:
forgive us our trespasses
as we forgive yours:
remember us in heaven
as clean scales and furs,
as we you on earth here
when any cat purrs.

26

XIV

Peter, salt Peter,
farewell and live,
        as we do remembering
and so forgive.

XV

        Over the whole world
a sad pall falls,
        fur into fine air,
bone into ash :
        a chill water
wets every lash.

XVI

        Peter, salt Peter,
by pleurisy slain,
        the pale glass weeps
in its wooden pane,
        come to the cat-flap
and slap in again.

XVII

        Peter, salt Peter,
the bird of death,
        a boding raven
chokes off my breath.

XVIII

        Wrung warm tears,
and doleful words
        end this dirge,
and the screams of birds.

c

THE SNOW LEOPARD

there is nowhere
left

for the snow leopard
stepping

down in the warmth
of a lying man

for a moment
except

in the glass ball
of his dream he

is dying
and

no-one knows
it except for

the man lying
in frozen state

on the white stone he
has entered

sanctified
and become

the

snow leopard
has awoken he stoops

in cold fire along
my breast-bone his

frost voice has risen
from the toils of ivy it

eases
his mane he

breathes in
the ice-swell

from the salt of his bowels his
madness is

green marble I feel
it sink

through bloody claws to
the skin

of my chest hollow and
chill

me and I am
his bone thoughts

frozen to
clothed silence

hearing
the night howl

in the stone he
is climbing now

crossing his paws
withdrawn to

those high shields
he started from where

my dream snows
foliating petals

crystal-sharp
claw-thin

dissolving
through icicles of tears

into cat-fur
poison ivy
                    the

snow leopard
has rested in

high silence he
blesses the

iron shields rusting
on stone he

returns there encircled
wreathed

and quiet
now

in the snows
of his dream.

IN THE DARK

1930s style

I

Past the clapboard
house. In his bent
white hat, he
walks.
        Dawdling. At
the window, naked,
she leans
out.
       Hey, there,
boy.
       As he turns
back from the car
door,
grinning.

II

       Ramming
her hot orange
into that fine
         close long
dress.
       (View up her legs
on the helter-skelter
down the wood
stairs.)

III

       Her hands, then,
grasping the
gun.

Stroking. Match
in his teeth,
rotating.
Over that huge
empty street.
(Rotundity of the
world.)
Running.

IV

Now
they are wrestling
on the hot
leather of the Cadillac.
He
twists
free.
Is out, and across
that hard grass, fingers
shaking.

V

Parting
her blond hair, opens
an ear, sexed
orifice.
In that first
bar.
*You're a
knock-out,* he says
later.

VI

And then that
elaborate, cool,
slow
scene

34

with the old man
in blue dungarees
and the negro.
           Bullets
from the .45 shattering
glass, shivering
wood.
           We rob
banks.

VII

           And then
their first job, abandoned
branch office.
                      You come out
there and tell
my girl.
           Acceleration. Wasted
bullets. Laughing.
                      The
dust rising
over the long
roads.

VIII

           And the gang
forming. *C. W.*
Moss, cap over
fat face.
                Buck.
Blanche.
           Time after
time, we go into
the same
                good clothes, *Good*
afternoon, ladies
and gentlemen,

                         this is
          the Barrow Gang.
                         And the cars.
          Racing. Over
          those flat roads,
                         flat out
          for Oklahoma.

                    IX

                    No
          breeze. Beside
          the road, the
          truck waits, the
                         old man,
          shifty in overalls,
          watching for them.
                         They
          drive along, eating
          apples.
                    He
          needs them, they
          get out.
                    Silence. She
          turns, he
          turns towards her.

                    X

                    And then
          that merciless
          beautiful
          perforation
                    of bullets, their
          bodies light, as
          if emptied,
          floating, trailed
          on the ground, from
          the car, pierced

'in
a thousand places'. The
vigilantes
           walking
slowly, not
sure yet.
           The noise
drying
into silence.

XI

           No, it is only
the projector
           hissing
in the empty cinema. They
lie, dissolved
in the wall, the
myth.
           Seeing
the green light
in the distance, the
                       dream
failing,
           ending
in the dark.

ON THE THUNERSEE

circa 1901

I

                    Meanwhile, the Baron Albert
Emil Otto von Parpart
rose from the left side
of his brass bed
and walked (first drawing
the curtains embroidered with blue thistles)
to the window, which he opened.
                                        Stepping through
onto a stone parapet, he stretched,
naked, in the cool air.
                        Across the lake
he could see the peak of Niesen,
above Spiez.
                It was a fine day.
                                Turning,
he re-entered his bedroom.

II

                            Meanwhile, his wife,
the Baroness Adelheid Sophie
Margaretta née von Bonstetten,
rose from the right side
of his brass bed,
which was also hers, and walked (first drawing
the curtains embroidered with blue thistles)
to her dressing-room.
                        There,
beneath a cylindrical, brass chandelier
fashioned with rosettes, she waited,
seated naked at her white dressing-table,
until such time as the Baron should have washed.
                                        (There was
only one bathroom.)

III

Meanwhile, the Baron,
having greeted the day, proceeded
to the glory of his ablutions.
Passing
through the first of several mahogany doors, he arrived
almost a little breathless,
on the upper level of his bathroom.
There he settled,
with some ceremony, his naked buttocks
on the lowered oak
of his English water-closet.
Evacuating
at his bare ease, the detritus of the evening's brilliance
into clear water, he rose
(as Christ) a second time, and flushed
what was left of himself
to the lake of Thun.
Through a linked series
of ingenious pipes, it fell
down forty feet of landscaped elegance
to amaze the perch.

IV

Meanwhile, the Baron,
unmindful of these metallic services,
bent down
to the sheet steel
of his hip-bath.
Kneeling in this,
as to the pew in their chapel his ancestors,
he absolved himself
with much grunting, and a little exercise,
of the body's dirt,
which is the sins of the flesh.
So cleansed,
upright at the mirror

above the hand-basin, in a white bath-robe,
the Baron shaved.
                         A little blood
flecked the marble
as he picked off some alert prominence
in the noble chin.
                         He dabbed
at the shorn skin.

V

            Meanwhile, his wife,
having thought over the day's impressing obligations,
containing her luxuriant wastes, as best she might,
on plaited cane,
grew restive.
                  He was longer than usual.
                                            She
sulked.

VI

            Meanwhile, the Baron,
having freed the temple of his deserts, the body,
of the night's adhesions,
descended to the second level
of his bathroom.
                  Throwing aside the bath-robe,
he began the slow process
of powdering himself.
                        Thereafter,
again naked,
he strode to his dressing-room.
                              On the glass-topped table,
beside his riding-boots,
a manual of Gymnastic Exercises lay open.
                                            He tugged
the tasselled bell-pull in the doorway
to inform his wife
her way was clear.

With a sigh, she moved,
at some speed, and in perfumed openness,
to the seat of her relief.

VII

Meanwhile, the Baron
(I draw a veil
over his wife's commensurate exertions, she was
no longer young)
extended his frame
in the morning lists of health.
So flushed
and bronzed, steeped
in a warm glow of remembered muscularity,
the Baron dressed.
As was his custom,
selecting without warrant of valet or chambermaids
the minimal tweeds
for the day's toilings, he hummed
a few bars of *La Bohème*, as he moved
between press and dressing-table.

VIII

Meanwhile, his wife,
now washed, and restored
to some fine ghost
of her former splendid narrowness, withdrew,
once more, to her dressing-room.
Whether maids,
masseurs, or her own mere sleight of hand,
had achieved such miracles as had been achieved,
discretion conceals.
In her clothes,
thrown on with care, though quickly,
she presented a firm spectacle.

IX

                              Meanwhile, the Baron,
returning in waxed magnificence
for the day's affrays,
humming and calm
passed through the curtains
embroidered with blue thistles.
                              Admiring his wife,
he kissed her.
                    Turning, he then strode,
with some purpose, and in high fettle,
along the mahogany corridor
towards the landing.
                         To his left he nodded
to his first Mucha,
a girl clothed, who drew
the sheet up to her coy neck.
                              To his right
he winked at his second Mucha,
a girl naked, who drew
the sheet down to her wanton waist.
                                    He felt
peckish.

X

                    Meanwhile, before him,
his double stairway with the wrought-iron flowers,
and the lamp-standards,
plunged like the Trummelbach Falls through its naked
    rock
towards the smell of kippers.
                              The Baron descended,
as do the angels, even, sometimes,
to the satisfaction of the fleshly appetites.
                              On the shell terrace,
in the sound of falling water,
the Baron attended, opening his letters
with an ivory paper-knife,

42

to all intents and purposes amused,
his wife's delayed arrival.
                              It was the year
of Jugendstil.
               A brooch by Lalique
drooped a florescence of contrived water-lilies
above his bending head.

XI

                    Meanwhile, his wife,
already tapping the yew balustrade in some distemper
with her manicured nails,
was on her way to join him.
                           Knowing this,
and the minutiae of her habits to the last detail,
the Baron rose.
               Ringing for breakfast,
he allowed the perfect Swiss clock of the world
to resume motion,
as it would continue to do,
without interruption,
for exactly thirteen years,
four months, and one day.
                         Knowing this, too, perhaps,
or having arranged it, as so many other things,
the Baron ate, without sparing,
cheese, rolls, marmalade, eggs, meat and honey-cake,
and, when he had finished,
wiped his mouth on his napkin,
belched, and, with a perfect conscience,
shot himself through the brain.

XII

                              Meanwhile, his wife,
the Baroness Adelheid Sophie
Margaretta née von Bonstetten,
having arrived, and eaten,

D

rose, and with a faint ruffle of her fastidious cuffs,
rang for the maid, who would, with some care
clear the table.

It was a fine day.

She opened her letters.

IV

TO AUTUMN

after Keats

I

Well, darling,
cock-teaser of
       old Mr
Hot-pants
with your fogged eyes, and
breasty look,
       don't tell *me*
you didn't plan
the whole bit with him,
       plastering
swags of bunchy
grape-fists over the lintel,
       dipping
shagged hawthorns with
gew-gaws,
       stuffing
au pairs with cream-cheese
et cetera,
       marrow-blowing,
nut-sucking,
       and generally
extravagantly exploding
nosegays
       under the velvet arses
of bum-boys,
       with a promise
it was all going
to keep on happening
       hot and strong,
musk-knickered,
       into the small
hours.

II

O.K.,
we know who
was threshed
          in the elevator,
coming all the way from the intersol
to the viewing-platform.
                 Also what
went on (or off)
that night behind the barn
in the stink of cow-shit,
                forked wide
for the queue in turtle-necks
after the May Ball.
            I've heard
how cool you kept
the long plungers,
              and those attentive
kitchen touches, draining
the beer-and-have-a-bash
boys.

III

Of course,
I take your point. They don't
all want
          the tarty sprig
in her first sprinkle,
             it's nice
once in a while
to get down
along the Embankment
              with the shepherd's
delight raging,
            shaved and randy,
and flick the stiff midges
out of your eyes
            beside the Needle,
gunning that sexy exhaust,

                           fetching off
the fresh chicks in the Wimpys,
eyeing straw blondes
                      in the clip-joints
and the odd busty old pro
in Lyle Street
                 from her top storey,
and then settling for you,
bitch-goddess,
                      under
the club-lights
respectable, sexy,
                   with a touch
of Rita Hayworth
a touch of mother and
a touch of Mata Hari
                      off to the South
soon for a winter
in bouncing Monte.

ODE TO A NIGHTINGALE

after Keats

I

All this flatulence, and
the pins and needles,
                    and then
to be turned off
like tipping *Harpic*
                    down
the *Humphrey*, well
it gets my goat. O I'm
not jealous,
                Flutterby,
it's just I see you
cooking all our gooses
when you open
                    that
big mouth of yours.

II

I need a *Pimm's*. Touch
of the old rabbit-food
                    out
of the freezer, smell
of the gay Flamenco, and
                    those hot sands
on the Costa. Or maybe
a jar
        of West Country
draught, fizzing,
with steaks in it,
                    and then
the quick fade-out
into the bushes.

50

I,II

Look, mate, you
don't know,
              what it's like :
crouched up all day long
over the in-trays
                  in the office :
bugged by rachitic
                  old bitches
and the starved look
of the Twiggys.
              I just
throw up every time
I stop to notice
              what with
all that smudged mascara, and
the music stopping,
              leaving
someone else stood up.

IV

Go on, I'll not
get stoned tonight.
              Sex
in the head, though,
              unknotting
opaque me
with gauze imaginings
as, e.g.,
              the
toothsome cool
of Lady Midnight,
              her bunch
of grapes in spangles,
bright fairies.
              Yes, but
not here

51

in the dim smoke
                   of the green-room
on the soft carpets.

V

    Here, it's more
the womb touch, all
Voysey papers,
                   and a drip
of joss-sticks, with a hint
of the usual
                   periodic
eccentricities : lichees,
green-sickness, and
                         prickling :
hemp and morning glory
seeds, with a few
                   well-drawn
puce groins by Rops,
not mentioning
                   those laid flagons
rich with cream
and hissed round
                   by the bar-flies.

VI

    You know
for years I've felt
I'd like to pack
                   the whole
thing in, even
written out
                   my famous
last words
about *melting*
into the world spirit
and so forth.
                   What with

you here
and it being all dim
                    and lively
I half-fancy
it for real.
            Just think,
to get hitched
with you in full flight
and me all comfortable
                        in
the alcove.
                It wouldn't work,
though.
            You'd soon turf
me out
        for dropping off
before your climax.

VII

    Anyway, you were
never the settling-in
sort.
        You've been around
a long time, flier.
                    Out
at Billy Smart's or the Palace,
in by the bulrushes,
fluttering hearts with
lashes,
        always
the open-eyed chick
who never grew up,
                    the new
bird from Frinton,
titivating the bay-windows
on the foreshore
                with a splash
of Eastern promise
and a breath of adventure.

VIII

Well, it was nice
while it lasted.
                    Here
at ground level,
grassed off,
it all feels
                    a bit
lorn, though.
                    I'm high
on half-truth
but she can't fool
me all
                    the time,
the tricksy pixy.
                    Don't
just go on flying
into the mean distance,
                                        up
the gennel,
                    tell
me if I'm
a liar
            or a lucky
bastard.
                    If I rub
my head, I
still hear
                    that Irish brogue
and see those green eyes
looking love-sick.
                                        So was
it for real
            or
am I (as the others all were)
up Shit Creek
without a compass?

ODE ON MELANCHOLY

after Keats

I

It's not a matter
of just forgetting
about it.
         Or wrenching
the caps off
aspirin-bottles.
              If you're
the awake sort, it
means, baby,
           the beloved
sinking feeling coming
a bit on the slow side, so
                 get wise,
don't start
messing about
           with
quacks and hocus-pocus,
death-watch, butterfly-kisses
of randy evangelists,
            or
fluff of Tengmalm, it
won't work.

II

Whenever you get
the heeby-jeebies, the
               creeps,
or whatever, like
thunder coming
             when you're out
without an umbrella,
clapping the hoods over

the wet leaves
in the whole garden,
grave-clothes
on your pet mountain,
the drill is
to work out on a Sarah Churchill,
or have a run
by the sea-side,
sit in with
packed vases.
If it's
your lady-love
giving you gyp,
the form is
get a hold of her
by the maulers, and
while
she has it off,
give her a tense glare
in
the pupils.

III

Remember, she's
the pretty one, it
can't last.
So turn
over in your mind
the gay wave you got
the last time,
and the nip
of orgasm, sour
even while they're
sucking off.
Yes, it's in
the whore-house,
there
in the back-parlour,
surrounded by the burst

sachets,
the mysterious
feather-boas, and
                    the call-sign,
splitting the
rhinoceros-pellets
                    between your teeth,
that's when
you get the final vision,
gasping your way
                    through
to where she straddles
                    in spent splendour
the chambers of impotence.

ODE ON A GRECIAN URN

after Keats

I

You're not
more than a fresh girl
in a cool church,
              now are
you ?
       Cross of a few
thousand centuries, and
not much noise,
             you
got your bland touch
with the country stuff
                (I grant
you, lusher than mine)
through lasting
           simply,
frocked with tree-myths
in ghost-fashion,
            gods
and us,
       and a garnish
of coy girls, lechers,
rape, riot, and
            the final
big O.

II

It's always
easier on the ear
not to have the
            music
actually *playing*.
         I

mean, if the oboe
tickles the fine roots
of the metaphysical
              man, not
the material one, you
draw a bonus.
           As,
for example, that
fine boy there
             in the clearing, he
won't ever get
what he's after, or
               see
(for that matter) the
leaves fall,
           but she'll
be as Camay-fresh
and desirable
             tomorrow, that
cool bint with
the Jimi Hendrix.

III

    Once you have
the consummation, it's
your swollen eyes, your
               morning
sickness and your Alka-
Seltzer.
         Whereas here,
I grant you, they're
all swinging, even
the vocalist,
         and
the trees.
         As for
those kids, warm
in each other's

E

           expectations,
aren't they just
having a ball,
                static
in glazed love,
and with all the new tunes !

IV

    Take the religious
piece, too.
             I agree
it's far better
from the cow's point
                of view,
not to be having
that funny boy with
                the dog-collar
really getting down
to his carve-up
                in the grove.
So she goes on
all smooth and flowery, and
                        mooing, too.
Then there's the bare city
beside the water,
                with the lynch-mob
all gone off to
their blood-letting,
                and not a soul
left with a bad story
to tell the sheriff
                about
where they are, and who with.
It helps, it
        helps.

V

Yes, you have
us all voting
for Miss Timeless,
                    the Greek
bird with the
curvy look.
                    She
has it all made,
the cold-as-marble look,
                    the few
twigs in her hair,
the down-trodden stance.
                              When we're
all grey, and fucked up,
(and it's coming)
                    you'll be there,
still charming, a mite cool
maybe, to our minds
                    in our troubles
but (and here's good news)
bearing the same message :
                              life's a bowl
of cherries, if you believe it,
if you believe it, life's
                    a bowl of cherries. That's
the big secret, man,
the only secret.

.

V

A CHRISTMAS RING

I   The Conception

On the first day of Christmas, when it snowed,
I lounged indoors, lulled by mulled wine, and read.
Then, I envisaged these sonnets, in a mode
Intricate as Mah Jongg. Monk-like, I sought what thread

I ought to sew with. Well, Biafra was owed
A delicate needle's care : some would have said
I ought to salute the Jordan, as it flowed
With blood, or see the starved in Christ were fed.

I know. It seemed an abuse of care to write
Only for Chinese pleasure, to pare time
In a warm room, seek themes out, switch on light,

And note swirled snow braking. Englazed in rhyme,
So much rang false. I heard the screech-owl creak,
Strafing each flake, immigrant to his beak.

II   The Pilgrimage

Strafing each flake, immigrant to his beak,
A stiff gull swooped. Light swanned along the lawn
On the second day of Christmas, glassily meek
Through snow-feathers. After a shepherd's dawn

Streaked in the East, a sheepish wind strayed, piq-
uant, smoke-filled. As I passed an oak-stump, sawn
For fire-wood in the park, it crossed me, reek
Of dried thorns burning. Was it meant to warn ?

A slush dome stretched in close, mist-ridden grey
Across England. Air changed. I felt it flay
My nostrils, eyes blear, feet slurred loose and slowed.

Suddenly, there were defences for this form.
A crisp sound echoed. Shanghaied through the storm,
A blackbird scattered his incense in the road.

III   The Annunciation

A blackbird scattered his incense in the road,
Welcoming me home. From communion blood I came,
Just before twelve, to my cleared snow. He showed
A blue-shot wing, and a bill of desperate flame,

As I stamped by him. Work slumped like a toad
On the third day of Christmas. I felt lame,
Hung-up, and guilty. Pride would need a goad
To start me composing, but this bird was game.

I set the pierced Yale to the jagged lock
And coughed indoors. The cold air zipped my brain.
Christ, it was that cat from next door again.

Look out, there, bird. As if to break my block,
With slow blows, he divided his gold Word. *Eeek!*
Max leapt to extol him, with a grief-hewn cheek.

IV   The Milk

Max leapt to extol him. With a grief-hewn cheek
On the fourth day of Christmas, dipping pots
In the cream of human kindness, as all week,
Our milkman smiled. Max camouflaged his spots.

O, Max is very sweet. Would never seek
To kill the Christ. Why, he licks babes in cots,
Is always gracious, gentle. Quite unique
Among the cats one knows, in knowing what's

What. Well, I see Max has one key to life,
Tuning his belfry of hunger, fly deceit,
And brazen for what he knows. He nudged my wife

Tenderly, filched some milk, then turned his feet
And tailed off. Life was a Ming episode,
Extending paws by water, where some flowed.

V   The Waste

Extending paws by water, where some flowed,
Max made me think of Asia. Near his drain,
I watched the waste rush. As he mewed and toed,
Life seemed a war. In Vietnam, as in Spain,

On the fifth day of Christmas, bombs would explode,
Rice straw burn, girls be raped, men slain,
And cats tease birds, and kill them. A cock crowed
For pagan Max in that red-spattered rain

Of soup, and tea, and peelings. Devilish, he
Savaged the gods in Bangkok, gulped the sea.
All flesh was grass. Each Himalayan peak

Melted in milk. Max hunched, then sprang at leaves,
Leaving me shaking blood-stock from my sleeves,
Hard by the drain-cope, red-specked from a leak.

VI   The Visitor

Hard by the drain-cope, red-specked, from a leak
A spider staggered. Along snow-swept stones
He stalked, circled in glory, as a freak
Ordained by nature. In my flu-stiff bones

I felt health squelching. Once, to some frail Greek,
He might have seemed a portent, fit for tones
Of grave thanks, weighty gnomes. I felt too weak
For such pre-Christian versing. Near the Nones,

All beasts were soporific. Awe-struck, ill
On the sixth day of Christmas from a chill,
I chose to praise a thrawn one, whose abode

Was a house of darkness. Flushed from pipes to work,
He swayed through waste. Eight legs blurred, vague in
  mirk
Where the tired crab-apple cleared its load.

VII   The Agony

Where the tired crab-apple cleared its load
Our hedgehog used to feed. Last summer, one
Night, as we talked in darkness, and heat mowed
And swept the terrace, I heard something stun

Stone, claw on concrete. By some branch's node
A strong foot seemed to grip. I thought, in fun,
Of Pindar's athletes. Then, as in an ode,
We found one squatting, quilled, and poised to run.

Well, on the seventh day of Christmas, milk
Might have been spread, with sogged bread, silk
In texture, and he might have stubbed home sleek.

That summer midnight he was carved in fear,
Hearing an owl. Today, from somewhere near,
I heard Christ's agony in the garden shriek.

VIII   The Crucifixion

I heard Christ's agony in the garden shriek
On the eighth day of Christmas, from his box,
Where he was coughing blood. A thorn-shaped streak
Of wet had mussed his back-fur. Muffled shocks,

Guns, firing on some serial, smoothed and chic,
Super-charged the horror. Listening clocks
In all the rooms made living seem oblique.
This was the killing-hour. Some came in smocks

With hammers, others with green liquids, wires,
And it was easy. All were penned, and killed.
Some by the crucifix, some trapped, and filled

68

With pheno-barbitone. A row of pyres
Blazed. I was where a small one's corpse was tossed.
Above his fur, snow-grey, the New Year crossed.

IX *The Resurrection*

Above his fur, snow-grey, the New Year crossed,
As Max walked out, and stroked things with his tail,
On the ninth day of Christmas. Coffin-mossed,
I dreamed about slain Peter. Like a snail,

I grieved a trail of glair for what was lost,
And made a wreath of shadows. Nail by nail,
I felt his box assembled, and embossed
With Christian fish. Outdoors, in sudden hail,

The garden flushed and rattled. Through a mist,
It seemed that there were green slides moving in
A sort of broken halo of red light.

I looked and wished. The watch-hands at my wrist
Shone for my cat, and all his living kin,
As, near its child, that nail-bright star by night.

X *The Love*

As, near its child, that nail-bright star by night,
So, in the morning, through a muggy fog
On the tenth day of Christmas there shone light
On Tabitha. She lay dumb, like a dog,

Along my Indian carpet, striped and slight,
Near to the fire. In her cat's catalogue
Few qualify, save Max. Max, in her sight,
Is as a brother, as he is. No clog

Sits closer to its foot, than Max to her.
She leaned, and slicked her tongue along his fur,
In Christian love. As Max rose, being Max,

And cuffed her, she cuffed him, then both made pax.
Writing, I smiled. Max cavorted, grey on white
Over the ice. On crisp leaves, Max trod light.

XI   The Ministry

Over the ice, on crisp leaves, Max trod light
On the eleventh day of Christmas. Near the flats,
Leaping, he sprayed. I laughed, and thought of tight,
Immaculate forms. If cats were all grey mats

On which to balance Chinese thoughts, one might
Spray to Confucius. Well, such spotless cats
As please the Lord must simulate his flight,
And rise to heaven. If men die like rats

In war and famine through the world, is verse,
Infected with such chronic cat-flu, worse
Than silence, prose? Well, what if it's not true

That a slash of cruel headlines nails you through?
Suppose, though, a brittle corpse does, burned, and
    tossed
Across a bald earth, graved in pewter frost?

XII   The Contrition

A cross, a bald earth. Graved in pewter frost,
On the twelfth day of Christmas, a girl came
To beg for Oxfam. For so small a cost,
How could I jib at helping? All the same,

Here was a hard sell. I felt pushed and bossed
Against my natural wax. I let the flame
Gutter along my cold staff, die enfossed,
And closed the door. Is, Murder, then, my name?

O, dear. To talk of writing because art
Means somehow coping, and then shrink from coins
Veiled in a box! Eating, I shivered. Sleet

Had been along the window, making part
More clean. Max came today, and coiled his loins
Near to where Tabitha strayed, smokily neat.

XIII   *The Betrayal*

Near to where Tabitha strayed, smokily neat,
Her brother hunted. In my pine, a bird,
The same that scattered incense, woke to the cheat
Of a warm day. As to the risen Word

In all His Glory, you could hear Max bleat,
Fleeced before March. In wolfskin boots, and furred,
He leapt be-knighted. As the ear to wheat,
Christ was a roaring flame. Deprived, Max heard

His clapper of derision ring loud and clear
Hosannas to the heights. Max had been near
To what he thought a special New Year's treat.

He purred in rage. Fingering down cards, I saw
Tabitha enter, gentle with tooth and claw
Under chrysanthemums. I heard Christ's wings beat.

XIV   *The Entombment*

Under chrysanthemums, I heard Christ's wings beat
When he fell black from heaven. On the ground,
Missionless, he was only so much meat
On a bird's bones. Where was that amber sound

That scorched the air, and hung there, like the heat
Of the last furnace ? Finished, in their mound,
October's thorns lay frozen. Down the street,
Starting, a jaguar rasped, rasped. Like a round,

I felt my poem snarl towards its end,
Swallowing Christ's wings. At Easter, would they bend
In restless flying ? To Tabitha he seemed

Motionless feathers. As she lay and dreamed,
I saw grey flakes, breaking to stall, implode
On the first day of Christmas, when it snowed.

XV   The Glory

*On the first day of Christmas, when it snowed,
Strafing each flake, immigrant to his beak,
A blackbird scattered his incense. In the road,
Max leapt to extol him, with a grief-hewn cheek,*

*Extending paws by water, where some flowed
Hard by the drain-cope. Red-specked from a leak,
Where the tired crab-apple cleared its load,
I heard Christ's agony in the garden shriek.*

*Above his fur, snow-grey, the New Year crossed,
As, near its child, that nail-bright star by night,
Over the ice. On crisp leaves, Max trod light*

*Across a bald earth, graved in pewter frost
Near to where Tabitha strayed, smokily neat
Under chrysanthemums. I heard Christ's wings beat.*

NOTES

I

A LIGHT IN WINTER: A middle-aged architect meets, falls in love with, and is left by, a much younger girl. Their relationship is born, consummated, and dies, between winter and winter.

II

THE SNOW LEOPARD: A man dreams of his dying cat. In the dream it becomes a snow leopard stepping down from an iron shield onto the rigid effigy of a crusader in a ruined church.

III

ON THE THUNERSEE: The bedroom suite described in this poem was installed at Castle Hünegg on the Thunersee in Switzerland in 1899. The names of the castle's owners are real, but the descriptions of their lives are fictitious.

IV

TO AUTUMN, etc.: These "distortions" are an attempt to extend the method of Lowell's *Imitations* to poems in one's own language. Readers wishing to make a comparison of texts may be helped to know that each section corresponds to one stanza of the Keats original.

V

A CHRISTMAS RING: The metre of this poem is a Hungarian one. I am grateful to Agnes Gergely for drawing my attention to it, with her poem *Johanna*.